# BRIGHT LIFE, ANIMAL HEART

# BRIGHT LIFE, ANIMAL HEART

Laura
**MINOR**

*For the women who keep fighting back*

Printed in the United States of America

ISBN: 979-8-9883272-3-3

Published by Conduit Books & Ephemera
788 Osceola Avenue
Saint Paul, Minnesota 55105
www.conduit.org

Book design by Scott Bruno/b graphic design

Distributed by Itasca Books
www.itascabooks.com

Cover images: *Portrait of Mrs. Maud Stevens Wagner, showing images tattooed on her upper body*, c. 1907. Courtesy Library of Congress. Additional photos courtesy Shutterstock.

# CONTENTS

*Only the devil can eat the devil out.*

—Sylvia Plath, “Witch Burning”

# BRIGHT LIFE, ANIMAL HEART

## For the Destruction

*All a poet can do today is warn*
—Wilfred Owen

Everything good and bad
done on this earth
is for love—

but how good it feels to be alone.

I've seen love step out, one model after another.

Our brains rewire with injury,
mid-gutter, piano falling—
my nail beds' pink fury,
against a cheek—
stay here,

cast to the soft blankets of the mind,
silver-print collisions as new daguerreotypes
till the discount gods burn candles inside us,
till the swinging lantern is engulfed.

## Witch, Hag, Crone

*You who were my only homeland, where am I going to look for you?*
*Perhaps in this poem that I am writing.*
—Alejandra Pizarnik

Like death, that smoke-filled jar
that sits on the forest floor—
home is sky, dirt, poetry.

I had to try and imagine a place:
Verge of green golden strobe
Corridor tap of hair and wood
Peaceful sorrow-fleshed globs.

Whoever drew these borders
can't see a shore yet—
and what stricken bet against the charcoal
unyielding in its violet strum of denim?

Transient as evolution's haunches—
women always know it,
those who move in concert, wizen,
holy against the crowned bog.

## Pandemic Romance Dream During a Sunrise Hurricane

The neighbor's employee is in the grass
grieving his own mother, distilling in the storm.
The ocean elopes from my arms,
its pearls grabbing him, me,
my cigarette out
on his expensive all-weather jacket—

my old Buick Regal and the sky's graying contract,
the morning silence blanched from within—

steamed by brightness,
iced by mercy.

For all our barnacles
fraught in their bohemian ensemble—
I waste myself by waking:

    hustling the dogs, grinding
    the beans, clicking mute

on our crushed Victorian lighthouse
now saturated with daybreak—

    two people who met
    and hushed it like a plague.

## Gratitude Poem with Swimming

I am thankful for the two-dollar avocado-themed pool float
I bought for the biggest moon,
        the last real one in forty years.

The pit, a removable beach ball—

we need each other, Robert Creeley,
we mustn't resist. Go on
with your gambling and your hot dice breath.
        Go on with your slingshot, too much
on the skull for existing—

        I'm thankful!
Tonight, I am David Berman of all poets,
and I want to remember his years' animal servitude

for this right leg that spins me left,
most goalless through the trees,
        and for the insects
        holding each other's feet.

### Adjunct

Queen of Homestead, Pennsylvania—

Margaret Mary Vojtko died face down
    on a street corner near her yard—

the world gathered its knitting languages
to her lap when she fell into
the root of all medieval texts.

I squeezed the bridge of my nose
until it was blue, wrote a song
about a woman, distant family,
dismembered by her partner. Such
service! To give your kicked shins
to the playground for bread and light,
barons free to take
our clothes from the trees' raked curls of sound.

    Cancer and twenty-five years in,
Margaret Mary went down,
        wandered out,
and died, discarded by her rented world
            of warbling tit-tots craning for their god.

The heart in service is a hatchet—
    dust for food.   Go on!

    We who live in the lace,
don't be fooled by security.
We smolder together—
    we scream the fire black.

## Black Clothes in a Pile

Past the green markets and electronic hope,
the mannequin leaning into the spotlight's beam,
the whole cascade of her
lit from above, the shoulders' lightning strike
        against galaxies' obsidian—
the city's promise of sleep.

Transplants surrender their drinks,
lessons learned, an asphalt blur,
eyeliner on a sham, the river-murk
mocking        *This is the show.*

The great ankle straps are wearing!
It's time to go home!

You'll soon be among the scavengers
of a different desert,

        but to close one eye
        on the train—
        hang on! The maw
        blows the pothole-lid high enough
        to hang your heels
        by the doting moon.

## Away from the Hustle-Hot Pavement

It was just a toast point on the earth's froth,
a reflection in the calico of the fire's aching brow.

Once owned by a sea captain
who remembered stories of bonnets
        neatly fastened under chins,
        broom handles' worn ends,
same salty pages
always folding in—
                water to water
                wave to wave
                foam to ignorant foam.

Away from the hustle-hot pavement
in a fist of wood near the beach—
        a kitchen bar like papaya flesh,
afternoon plump as a sea scallop
bound and doused on the grill
with a solitary peach-squeeze,
the juice sweetening the sea glass path
to the outdoor shower, where stilled,
our minds thought of nothing's cosmic tug.

Self-exiled by the need of other, wonder
the choir of aperture,
        the ocean's forever groan.

## Apples for Adrienne Shelley

Blonde with a smear of Phoebus rising—
sour sweet and deep in the fall—
        the first organic apples.

        Two women handing out samples,
evolution cradled in artisanal baskets
full of a weekend's city shoppers.

We discussed film
when no one would stop by the stall.
Until one day, Adrienne Shelley,
        now an auteur
with her signature frames and cardigan,
stopped and we cooled ourselves
like we didn't know who she was.

She appreciated us not giving it away,
mocked organics along with us,
then slipped away into the crowd—

a hole in the day where nothing
as sensational would happen again.

Shade deflated into thin wedges,
how much the fall scene from *Trust*
taught us about love, and the letter
of motherly pie-making
written for her daughter.

We tried to fill the hole
for days and then
we were, one day, different people
with better jobs and she was
murdered in her shower—

space, fathomless,
elastic with neon.

## She Is the *Least Changed*

On the way home, my father bought
my mother a novel, a romance novel
from Winn Dixie, and shortly after,
the house fell apart like a putrid fruit,
and hidden jewelry never fell from the pages
        on mom's fortieth.

Who is the mother's birthday
that everyone remembers?
A mother's birthday,
a thorn
in the back pocket.

        Desperate renovations would begin in the rain.
Newly made pictures in haste,
        grief cutlets under a blouse,
posing in the bread aisle, or on a homecoming float in 1965,
ankles crossed by time's milk jug picket fence.

At the twentieth high school reunion,
she was awarded a coffee mug:
*Least Changed.*

I asked her what that meant, and she said it meant that she
*looked most like her high school self. You know, not fat.*

Women
age past ten, forty, and get a mug—

their futures small, adolescent in captivity,
while the rest get to morph into their last bodies,
wave comfortably from outside of the jar.

If you ask her
of resilience

she will become infinity, curl
into a hair roller tossed in the cup holder of a CRX hatchback,

her first new car. She will grip the phantom wheel
of her younger mane
undulating in real time like a mudslide,
like oil spilled
in a moment of ecstasy.

## Kindness Yet

*For auld lang syne*
—Robert Burns

Late, in the consistent Bossa Nova repair,

our childish days freshly dressed—

we ready the bedcovers
for what good awaits, what more—

cheer's meek acquiesce.

I remember love,
my whiff of body asleep—
flare folded into pitch.

Our lives, vine-slick
with dollhouse rot.

I flick my forgiveness. This year
was stupid with buildings—
all the windows
caught fire in my gaze.

## Famous Writer in the Dojo Gives Me Hope

A tired star-in-training, I crumpled my food bag,
and stared at myself from outside this dojo window,
thinking what I hope *he* was thinking—it's go time! Kick!

We're both the raunchy panhandle patois
we were born to be. I knew when I met him
eventually, but as a singer, unbuckling oysters
with new students gathered around a farm table,
unlikely ambassadors for the hawks and raccoons—
our country was
        the country of do-over.
To champion a shiny, new narrative,
        kick back against the new kids,
the old brown booze, the ex-wife's eyes—
blueberries run-through the teeth of another day—kick!

He was throwing his legs and torso around
for another chance or a woman, some life left
at the end of the punches. And I'm watching him
hit back and it's getting hot and I'm as dewy
as any sun-brewed brow—
        I'm watching him, me, all the comeback kids.
sparring with the strip mall of life,
        to be
        *in perpetual start*—kick!
In love with survival and self,
in love, the belly warmed with new chances,
in love, the concave hunger
        of every last page—kick!

## Cousin Pam & the Want Ads

He came to me recently,
the man from the personal ads in 1995.
My second cousin was a friendless lesbian,
and I said *I would*
if *she did*. She was
never well, but tender as a stranger hug
despite the usual Parliaments and fried okra
for breakfast. She set me up with a job
caring for her ex with MS
who once pushed me
out of the way to see a starlet on tv.

Scott, the date, was okay,
a metal screen print artist who liked *The Simpsons*
and had a goatee. I was scared and young,
but extremely curious about others.

I went. I want to trust,
and he was quite nice,
took me to meet his friends
down the street. They
were on meth, and the rooms
were unnerved gales. A woman
with two front teeth missing—
a blowjob joke I didn't fully get.
A man who pulled his shorts aside
in the hallway to illustrate his
nudist beach, *Black's Beach?*
He was tan.

Back to Scott's house, I had to ask
about his armoire, two engraved metal
panels, a lock. He asked me

if I was sure. I wasn't
sure. It was filled with sex toys
I'd never seen before. I asked

about something like a jewelry pouch.
He told me that you pull the string
tight to make it hurt.

I said something along the lines
of getting back, her loneliness,
my newness to everything.

I left and went to find my car.
I must've parked down the block,
and even in a small California suburb,

I was lost—until
I was in a sunflower garden
someone must've grown
for the gullible believers of love,
sanctum spikes still trusting the light.

## Shooting

On the inside of his collar, a red collar,
a "God-don't-leave-this-place-collar,"
awkward with the cha-cha of libation and libido
that sticks its landing like the gluey sickle
of a fake eyelash. You never want

a lover's birthday to fall on a town's misery,
unless the only thing that helps
is someone's animated body against your own.

I am the woman with hopeful earrings and lipstick
talking to a man we've come to celebrate.

My rascally roommate leans into beau number two.
It is the everyday stuff of bars, except

I am a woman without a gun
and some kid just shot up our university library
on an otherwise lazy weekday afternoon.

Later, I will crawl into the cab of my truck
with the man to smoke away the heat
still escaping our slow dance—

the straggling barflies
give up fighting the ghastly parts of the night.

The talk of America and guns
comes to an impasse
like the shooter's mind,
now retired from its terrible occupation.

And now, dragging myself home
to a couple of jackets thrown on a chair
barely touching each other,
        the roommate's carnal chuckle
        from behind the drywall—
I stare at the jackets thrown,
that sliver of space,                    Death

as it lines up your jaw
like slippers for the morning floor.

In bed, I text a colleague for that Frank O'Hara.
I asked how we                                        need it
as much as we    want it:                 art, lovers—

all the misfires of the day throw whiskey
down the curve of my throat—

## Last Desert

The ecstasy: water, wine—

compounds leading to vows,
implosions in the chest's matchbook.

And here I am, stuck
between this uncertain afternoon,

this sagging couch cushion, this
sand-worn bra drowned as the desert.

Before I go on
becoming properly wise, a self-portrait!

A jowl-bloodied vase, some vulture
fluted with the evening's flower—

and now, some water
to comb out the mane
of my own ranched Pegasus
that has galloped down my skull to tell me
I no longer need
or think I deserve,
        the deep's intent to drown me.

## Passing a Woman on the Way to Work

A wild fang of her hair eats the rain,
down the train platform, down the iron stairs—

she hurriedly guides her toddler down
into the sleepy burn—

every woman's shoulder
as they push through
to the next family photo, the next
touch, mystical revelation, sweet
on the tongue—
        life's storefront grate
unsound as the next day's sun.

                    Once again in my seat,
            grateful for this bruised locomotive
        that hauls women and their granules

of fiery, manageable rage that power the planet—

        the people around me steady their books.

## Three Girls

O to be on a dance floor
filled again, mascara with tequila,
        hair in speaker,
clovered crowns, snatched cosmos—
save us now

as we round our bodies
into more sensible clothes
sensible houses—
        no dancing in sight.

What is it about a girl
        with a license to break open the earth?
We could have thrown men to the gators,
        drove dogs to Canada.

When we move now,
        it's alone,
forever glommed,
the divine bass as laughter
        reignited in the great diagram.

## Libidinous Cherry

*Stuck on the same landscape,*
*close to her, as if it grew*
*in her own mouth.* Look at my feet—
I would set them on fire to see that red again.

I am here in a glass soldier nation
writing you in hairs across the bar.

Old composite—
you make everything
as mysterious as the seafloor at dawn,
everything a borderless new countryside
        whining into the drink.

I take out the garbage, do the dishes in the bathtub.
The mail comes, the money,                    more or less,
        flips by like a subway read.

Suddenly, prose
        becomes a necklace of plums,
a character constructed from a pebble on the highway—
more questions of the abundance in us. I make
turnstiles from my appetite, sewing lines
with my tongue, stories—
        the only heaven.

We are vicious,
muscled in our armor—
only a few strands away
from the great American novel!

*She yanked the beer to her crotch*
*and dreamt of a world three cities*
*ago, the strange walls clipping her hair*
*as she knotted it with quick jabs,*
*girls fencing across the sun.*

## The Day Bowie Died

Tonight, your image in the room,
thinking back on the afternoon
when you broke it off, the day
that Bowie died, our
only anniversary—
        I still keep you in my side eye
        like neglected laundry, carry you
        like knuckles, wear your uselessness
        like a hood ornament—
but, if I could say one last thing,
I would tell you that the mystery left in you
could drown a jellyfish, prevent
the birth of a colt, or something.
Even though you could complain
about the trees ignoring you
when you walked by,
        I would reassure you:
even youth leaves us like gold curtains
                                                landing on the ground.
I knew fire was my destiny, not yours,
a slow drag burning—the red coal of what it is
to exist in the same room with no one else.

You bumped over the boiling water and coffee grounds,
        and it slid down my leg,
                our only anniversary—
a red lightning bolt across my calf.

## Cambodian Snake Wine

One ruptured year, I fell for an old friend,
        kindling ready to reignite,
freshly divorced and after me again.
A night out, stiff with time
ready to strike—
        Cambodian snake wine!
Petrified in its ship, I drank to that!
To those venomous prisons-—
        now        is the drugged crow of my gaze!
        now        is my bread and butter!

This is the pocked elegy
for that year spent in L.A., rudderless,

him punching the dash of our F-150—
        I shirked my only religion, put the calling on hold—
        the small employment—
never to skulk back to warm milk
in lieu of poems.        People shake hands,
show their congeniality, the inflammable talk
sloughs off, a swig of something rag-thin
that snakes your dreams,
crawls up your midnight leg—
        a prayer's lint
and not the prayer itself!

## Bright Life, Animal Heart

for Sheri Lynn

You knew the etymology for morphine and doorway,
how bathwater holds children like minnows,
how to drive a silver Cougar
with your tune-injected tan,
voice between mermaid and human,
flipping your hair at fate
while pink bubblegum rolled your tongue
and a constellation of freckles
threw a net to the sea.

For the world that will not yet allow me to rinse into blackness,
for your gravestone somewhere in Florida
that sticks up like a finger in the bathtub,
I stand in the doorway as it crumbles.
I do everything the sky requires of me.
The river stones are turning into women
who pound, thump—animals left to lord
over the howl and estrangement of this hunt:
an arcade of salvation
or tender horn to the animal of death?

## Gratitude Poem for One of Us

for Jane Mead, after Jean Valentine's poem for Jane Kenyon

the poet who died yesterday—her work, I can see
the final fray      in crescents and rasps—
Jane. I can blubber

for her—Jane—on the quad,
the campus fountain I discovered
with co-eds cast in stone
hiking their masonry skirts
to play in the main—

their blueprints under our poems
          the way this fountain atomizes anyone
gone,      never gone,      evaporated
refreshed of the universe—

this fountain screams *J's*—
          Janes,
all of us,
          fishhooks in the spray.

## Because It Is Bitter, and Because It Is My Heart

after Stephen Crane

I can't remember who I am under these ribs.
When I turn, suddenly, or move wrong
my body has a cramp, like my rib is stuck
on something that grew inside
when my back was turned.

I go away and sing songs, write poems
for betterment: always act, always stand up.

I go back in, set the park on fire, say
*Get in the car!* and we head straight for Mexico
the shrimp villages, just an hour over the border

stop in Tecate for street tacos
see rusted wrecks blossoming
a cliff's rocky ankles, no guard rails
in sight and this is when

I apologize—we both know
I've let myself go.

I no longer want to be attractive
and it slips in with a long breath
in our silent reunion—
nothing by design.

For someone or thing
that shook my middle—

and there it is
still with me
through these homicidal times.

## Metamorphosis, Unfolding

This was a kindergarten
where across the river,
the Twin Towers still stood.
Our butterflies were raised, named,

and I said,          got away—

a pigeon through the limbs,
confetti-whipped carnage—spirits
jitter-hopping the tax.

But children are quick, coated
in the quartz rain of membranous bits—

abuse from another's world
cycled back into the leaves' fragmented misery,

gauze picked up by the wind,
the sky—
death-warrant pastel.

## Carpet Shark

I've finally had enough.
Mount them on the seawall,
breathe back
their dusty cave marks,
dwell in taxidermy
for the masses of women
still plagued as *devil,*

as if every woman hasn't known
hunter versus the hunted

the ruse of pageantry
the spoil of torch and hiss
*seductr ess temptr ess.*

That torture sinks cities,
tears the sky like a finger across a throat.

Suck these jailers into the black holes they fear.
Spit them out like postured fluff,
buoyed creatures in all their exodus,
trophy sons now chum
in the gulf theater of justice—
the vaudeville of every woman's life.

## A Copy of *Diving into the Wreck*

It shoots out like a ninja star,

like the time I talked to my aunt,
a landlord, about one of her renters—
a woman's husband died
from drinking too much, this time
a bottle of rubbing alcohol,
somehow,        the woman said,

into the light with her jaw wired shut
behind a screen door. It flew
across the room
and stuck in the wall
like a machete in a watermelon.

I got the feminist power fist tattoo
on my arm shortly after—
I said it was to remind myself to always
make feminist choices.

But I didn't always make feminist choices.

My models and their contradictions
hovered over my life remote, and I moved
out for a short while at sixteen, where
I was raped by a cruise worker visiting town.

But I know the women in my life
have been raped, and for a moment there
the meander of bad men continued,
and if that confuses you,
you don't know much about rape.
And now, I have to do all this
struggle and shame
        even with the tattoo. How
can we go on like this?

I dove in, and it's good. It's there
because I need it, the work of diving—

just the work
        over and over again.

## Neighbor Held Captive, Stabs Boyfriend Four Times in a Death Spiral

A famine begins in the road's wound,
the blood snow abandons light's unopened letter
before dawn wipes away her first wolf moon,
and trucks point like arrows drawn back.

The blizzard warns the forest
free as the mulberry wine forth from his neck.
Their love trades possession for tragedy's couture—
the mountain trailer,
the stenciled porch signage about the heart,
the little dog's bowl,
the deer-head cape in the yard.

I see her after the mess of it—
in the fresh turf laying garden stones
selling walking sticks, etchings—
her sleeping pills now headed out to sea.

Her boyfriend will smash her newest phone again,
raze the rib's air cage, but she
was my warrior.

## Dinner Party

I left my contacts marinating in the shot glass above the toilet
my eyeballs yellowing on the windowsill
my breasts speared on the tines of your fork
my jawbone cocked open in the miso
my waist bent on the brim of a bowl
my head hanging limp over the rug
—and my lips strained and white in the colander—
I left my fingers cooling on the stove
my shin bones swept in the dustpan
my forearms in the kindling, my collarbone
licked clean by the dog
my shoulder blades scooped in the spinach dip
my lashes gathered in the gutter of your plate
—and my vertebrae stir-fried with orange pieces—
I left my tongue bobbing in the wine
my wrists, holding toothpicks in a bloom
next to the tiny bones of my hands
spelling *feed me* on the good tablecloth.

## What to Do with the Brutes

Greased piglets hotfooting a pen—
*I'mma get em for ya daddy—*

as they descend from our grasps,
freed from country sport.          Children
were there to get dirty,
never to possess,          abuse—
                    except for a few—

        the ones I want to pen now,
        the ones who knew play
        but leaned a cruel way
        to feel the oar's favor.

I would take them all over the side
and feed them their ogre hearts turned terrible hydra.

Then, to groom          them,
sweet as berried cream, yoke them
to my cart, and ask
        *Where is it that you call home?*

They will think hard.
They will take me to see their best memories,
where no one brutalizes the garden, no one
        chases you while you thrive, no one

                                        in the chorus of gunslinger and thief
                                        is caught in their own milling of mules
                                                tethered to the creaking wheel.

## Undo

for Virginia Woolf by way of a dream delivery service

Drop your hands to the river, *Ouse*,
drop the stones into the muddy river, drop
the river, drop the mudstones at the mud-
bottom, laugh, become brackish in escape!

The overcast trickle of abyss
the ink, the air, the wing
the algae dripping mud—
        strike first
and strike hard at the bank head savior!

Reverse your path, the room, the river
spit yourself out, unfurl—

and dutiful dunes ride you back
to your favorite chair, ginger, and tea,
pen-cup priestess, scribe of consequence!

## The Talented Rapes of Our Time

Recently, my rapist flew into the room,
a slick pilot, served low-country boil
with a colonizer's smirk—

chicken wings served up with a guttery drip.

No one minds

a gulping rapist. I cried myself radioactive—
        peacock of pain! My rapist
multiplied into two teenagers
in a dorm room picked clean of lies,
but they soon grew awkward, bored.

But my rapes keep making it through the day!
One boyfriend on a film channel reality show—
night-blue horror, jolting my slumbering mannequin
        into undrinkable armor.

My cousin told me about the boys
who pulled her off her skateboard, failed
as she slipped away on foot, never got the chance
to rob a life, lodge a metal toothpick in her spine—
                        and still, she had to see them
        in school, opening their math books.
Don't look away. It's one of your favorites.

Supermarkets, conferences,
dinner parties with their girlfriends,
wives—brocade in their ceremony.
Rapes are nothing like supernatural hedges.
My rapists had money, college, and eventually,
wee children to protect
        against the world's rapists.

My last rapist was still blossoming his reach
just after the first tree dropped its inaugural petals
        into spring's spiked jowls.

None of my rapists have ever heard me sing.
None of my rapists were able to crawl inside
        my cabbage heart unfurling. I regenerated,

which takes real power,

to rise slick with residue birth—
in the dark,
        be the Volta and forgive
the stars' fetal rage.

## Napalm Death, 1997

When I was young and new to the city,
the people I met thought of me as a great story,
a peach for a bartender's pupil—
        Say        *Banana*
and then,
        *Listen to the twang*
                        *on this one—*

I'd never thought of myself as some Panhandled,
ham-fisted girl, but the mixture of want
for an education and the wild champagne
pop of the south, compelled me
to Zelda up the coast into my royal blue,
newly converted elevator shaft, the iris of a loft,
where freshly powdered roommates
dragged me in front of a band,
        and in the audience,
a neck: not tragic, just older.

I saw myself in a New York woman's neck—
        a neck the color of soured moon glow,
Millay's ivory dildo with notes of whalebone—

beginning to show the signs of aging, something
we never see coming, something that begs the question:
        *How would I earn that look in this city?*

I went home thinking about the lead singer,
a broken messenger. He looked tired
and slightly bored
        as if to say:
        *I'm a poodle on two legs.*
        *I'm a jokey postcard.*
I thought of that woman
who would soon fade from my ongoing story—
        that slick honeycomb of New York,
        men always like an octopus.

Then, one day I woke up
        and all my friends were frustrated versions
of what they cared about in the first place.

Now, back in the Gulf city of my youth
running the length of a dock withering
under my gait, trying to build a home
in someone else's gaze—

        I sit in this LabCorp room
waiting for my blood work—

I used to want to be the kind of woman
        who balked at naiveté,
                ate men like mangoes
and threw the peels over her shoulder.

Finally, woman in the club was on the Bowery
in a black dress, alone,
watching these same guys
from her heyday, silent—

sustaining is in everything,
        even your baby pictures.

To a few outlaw years—
we, who can do nothing,
lean-in for who we were,
or thought we were—

        and what do I know from the new sounds—

when all the burning castles
        settle at once.

## A Marriage Contract

I frantically shake the void
like a bottle of divorced juice—

glasses on my head.

## Big Dick, Small Town, I Love You, Now Show Me Your Tits

If Sunday was a man, he'd be good,
not the scourge of wooden hours—
some digital acquaintance, a high,
friend, superior, colleague, or mentor
ruefully horny, delusional on their own back roads
something to explain away uncurbed behavior
a warning shot
before the show can begin
texting me at dawn just as I began
grind the grind down
my morning tango to the coffee smell.
until you're trapped,
He doesn't want to deny it anymore.
He says he has a real thing for me

two people sitting alone in a park
waiting for some music
*You know—big dick/small town*
*Show me your tits?*

open air, no echo
no one to help hear
words meant to
silence
entice
only the birds and worms know—
First, I think it's funny.
a moment to scorch the bog
and spray others with his failed years' mud.
He doesn't think I'm human! He thinks
he's texting a food order.
It was a cheap shot with the breeze.
But I believe him when he says he's a painter
and doesn't understand words as much as images.

Keep it, lose your shame
to someone who refreshes your life
with new laughter and children, someone
to walk in and need you
after you've worried the coals bare—

I tuck the phone in my bathrobe pocket
that is bunched together by my elbows

*we* are not comfortable enough
to brandish ourselves like beer stalls

to burden the mosquitoes—

I'm hoping he gets distracted,
clean clothes for another day.
But the high is strong,
and he has miles to go, so he calls.

annoying in their attempts
to chip away at brazen.

He's talking fast, saying fast things,
as if *I Love You* was speeding in the car next to him
racing to connect him with his best moments—

Instead, give us both daystar, breath,
a pause before we speak,

a brief tilt before life's diorama nosedives

some care for the hours ahead
in the violent trigger of grass—

music forgives us, again

and falls headlong down this hillside.

## Plan B

Fear is a thing of acid and tears
cauterizing the womb

a red pen knife, a bottle of the pink stuff
to wash down      a parking lot on fire
        a car seat      there?
        an oxygenated prayer
a future without      with
more      what I want            air

        another woman peering
at the sight of me arrested with last chances
the comfort of my jean jacket
tying me to the steering wheel—
women know
        when women sit in cars—
        the way we read a clock

nervous smiles, hands scoring time
        a dial
              every stomach exposed.

### Decade

out of shock one night in a favorite bar
the sadism of several martinis
a friend jazz-handing trivia
while    flanked by strangers
I downed them like swords

and this is when I listicle the terror-scroll    as the DJ taps out
        target    rape    torture    gaslight    smear
    the faders weave between
            unalive    prison    death    disease
till the bad actors drop in their gowns
till the backup dancers fan out in their rotten bouquets    I'm tired

of humans        we're supposed to be citizens, neighbors
not performative cage matches    creeps deep in this scam
this scab of years

    another friend's husband
    who shoved his hand down my pants
    while I was asleep
            also supposed to be my friend, citizen, neighbor
haters  elders  family  doctors    gossipers    willfully indifferent
    impoverished voyeurs
all supposed to be        friends
same friends  who left this world
you should've stayed
    same friends        who died
be there still    send me signs    often

we must make more music
travel        write all the time

busy heart        you made it through
the roughest one
I can’t imagine this life or that death

one decade

## Ghost Ocean

*My body has experienced your great punishment.*
*Lament, bitterness, sleeplessness, distress, separation...*
*mercy, compassion, care,*
*Lenience, and homage are yours, and to cause flooding, to open*
*hard ground and to turn*
*Darkness into light.*
—Enheduanna, *The Hymn to Inanna*

Never nasty, good/bad girl,
measured almonds, bird-like, never
sage, skirt, four-eyed unwed birthing
house, duvet, never divan, dinner
companion, never captive wildcat in-waiting,
never nails slightly over, never rose, Rosé,
epistolary illusion, never choke, never ice,
never cackle, never red, never the gray
sweat-suited grunt, never cucumber-
eyed monsters, tappa tappa flamingo pink
crinoline, never inspirational quotes, never
a bet, Bettie, never never never muse,
never a reservoir for your ribbed pleasure, never
who'd you rather, never off-the-shoulder,
never carried, never serendipitous, never party girl,
never shrew, never teacher, never
your age, never yoga pants, never slut,
never fruit cup, never walk of shame,
cheerleader, nymph in the reeds, on
a rock, on a boat, in the air, on a broom,
inhabiting a cat, witchy woman, evil/woman, bad
girls will always be bad girls, uptown/downtown
girl, girl with the curl, never on the rag, PMS,
track her chart, eligible, not
eligible, calculating,
never conniving, never
Spanx, never sacrifice,

never baby, never war/bride,
magical kitchen, whirring toasters,
never *mattress*, quiet passion, bright star, never
color block suit monster, never first wife,
never breeder, spinster, barren,
user, never never gold-digger,
never my mother used to make it like,
sharp-tongued, corseted, brainy,
claws on chain link fence, never lipstick
on the mirror goodbye, never locked-
in, never she's good          but, she didn't do it
herself, never the bass
player, singer, band girl,
bad girl, never say
lady without first saying
lord, never panties-in-a-wad, never
horse, pig, bruiser, whale, compliment,
ornament, troublemaker, man-taker, home-breaker, never
pantomime horse, the fatale floating
frond up,
pond-clear,

never.

The membrane oozes
a predictable litany, first, that
bobble-headed myth
knocking the small walls
opens the book again,

*The Longest Revolution*,
again—

it's still in your mind,
pressing the crevices—
tearing out the pages,
kicking out the ladder

        and rise        rising—

I brush the soot from Aurora Leigh's feet,
and chant as them before me
scatter in the shush—
        Enheduanna
                Nanna, Inanna—

I pull the rest of them up: Faltonia,
Helen of Egypt,
Seward's dead cat,
little Annie Allen,
those womanly Argonauts,
Odysseans, writers of epic—
each one floating up
                the old bone ladder.

I straddle this maritime wormhole,
surfaced junkyard window to the lost.
I pull up their names
to untether
        aquanauts from their ledgers,
priestesses from their scribes, burn
their seals and scream the sky's brutality.

## Dinner Party II

The forks teeter on the edge of the table,
        the cage of their tiny ironwork
gathered after the holiday party,
        the blue screen of the TV to the far left
like a stained-glass portal to an ocean beyond.

The guests flit about the mess
shuffling from room to room
        clearing plates, mournful
about the one who isn't well, happy
        for the babies and talk of dogs.
The clinking is pierced
by the cackle of old sisters
        loudly over the mechanisms of feet.

I go to the living room, sit squarely on the couch
hoping they all might follow suit, but it's time
for naps and commutes across town. I feel
like falling over and then rolling
                off the couch into a corpse pose.
All their well-wishes in passing whispers:

*I just know your book is going to do well.*

*Have you heard anything back yet honey?*

I remember the postal worker a week ago
with the salutation, *You have to start somewhere!*

Everyone has left,
but the walls can see
the red table runner
sliding down my mouth
into the wrinkled tree
growing between my breasts.

Pick up your life,
this crooked murmuration of days.
The champagne stem tulips you back
into the universe. I put it in my mouth,
shove it in with my country thumb,
and chew.

## Casting for Suppleburgers

to Allison on her 50th

It's your natal day during the plague
and the feast of your future years melts
the sponsor of the moon, crisps the buttery sun—
when we are now at the middle of our time

free air—

I hold your arms up in a too-tall world.
I see your goodness crumble the pavement
and the windows go up around you.
The trees odalisque across the city
to salute you in their leggy tributes.
The universe made you
so we would never forget
the prism of one life,

our favorite names
like diamond combustions—

*Allison*, ssh
little roasted fishes in the leaves
little parsley cap on the sea
doxy of egg & sashimi shimmy
Sake cop! True-crime hosiery
and little pesto popper—Allison!
Thumbelina's crystal bell
lemon chickenatta—
my one and only suppleburger.

Over the years, us shrinking guttersnipes
will burn in the shine off your white boots walking,
scuffed goddesses weaving concrete legends.

## Fist Fight at the Golden Corral

We open with forgiveness—
my friend who almost left this world
by diving out of a second story
with an amplifier cord
wrapped around his neck
which broke, and he fell headfirst
into broken bits of concrete
to the tune of jawbone and wire
and learned to speak and move
in a rot of months until well enough
to rejoin the world and trade air
with us once again, lean into the scrap
and gorge of life's greatest trough,
The Golden Corral,
where he would eat away his childhood evictions,
the impoverishment of parents, the abundance
of stepmoms and comic books, the strippers
of a sterling thirteenth birthday,
a horseback tit-in-mouth surprise
where a boy would grow into a man
defending a mother at the cash register
who wanted more crab legs, more shrimp,
more horn for the cornucopia
of a chocolate syrup fountain
and was punched in the eye
by the small owner after reaching over the register
to deliver a comically grave slap—
chicken wings flying in the deeply broken world
of sweet corn pudding seeking pardon
from the Italian pasta bake and cinnamon apples,
the fried fish asking the pumpkin pie
to never end, never give up.
We are all the last three pieces of nothingness
flung from a tray

on the violence of linoleum
on a much-needed weekend paradise
of beans greening the communal peace.

## Sea City

I've invented an animal for you
who I groom with a coral comb.

Spare your ships the irascible tracks
of my chariot as this pony hoofs
irreverent donuts into your soil
and your beleaguered freeway travelers
call upon the withering drifts
like women bent over bathtubs
to rise and dome you over—

we must become the visionaries of Atlantis.

Lift slowly to strike out at nothing except peace
and meet at the old jean-shorted scrap of sand
where shark fishermen throw their minds to the sea
and surfers shred the skyline like dragonflies.

        You are not yet a fighter!

Blood still bubbles over Matanzas
where whole families were slaughtered
by families who slaughtered more families
in the machinery of inlet,
dinghies high on dock wood
and the memory of manatees—
        you are more than a land of end-zone gladiators,
        flip-flopped believers, eaters of shirtsleeves.
        See how the river's dirty fingers
dig into my oceanic margins?
        You are not whole yet.

Give yourself over to the young.
Your children will inherit mountains
of Meyer lemons—
        though you get no vote,
        I want to caress you again.

Water is the greatest equalizer,
as a dreaming boy artist with a sword
tattooed under one eye paints you
        the color of blood oranges in cream.

## Night Dishes

The drugstore was ragwork in its wishing.
The mechanic bowed the clock over the motor.
Even my doctor's car was humping the speed bump.

And I was alone, again, with my breath.

The dishes were there
sliding and smashing into each other
without care for odor or dirt,
ready to cut
or break
in their murky juices.

## Give Mom My Projector Dream

From the safety of my palatial spacesuit, I'm numb
        to the lust I once cycled like a college town—
forever forever college town
        where I learned to fight for everyone, but first,
for women underfoot.

I gave my all like a leaky lunchbox, the lore
dribbling my stories into the pocked sidewalks of feral cats
where I transgressed beyond one boyfriend's book on ships.

They never tell you
college towns are a possessed bloom of bruises to pluck.

If you get separated from your youthful self, go to water,
your dream-tattered jalopy of time-travel,

back to when you were a swimmer,
back to the surf, the days of art modeling,
when your mom threw away the best drawing, even though
it was only from the shoulders up,
and you remember that day because Egon Schiele's paintings
were projected over your muscles
while you tried to memorize *Song of Myself*
taped to the wall that held your eyeball,
water moving around and through
people—dying, wanting,
trying, which now, looks like
all the dampened embers of sets finishing like campfires.
I still want my mind here, there—
people and their songs.

This is when I disrupt myself gently
like a wet glass found in the bushes
after the party has ended, hand-dry
those days against the wrist's soft slope—
        old towns, like women, change
with the measured wait for their story
        in the attendant blades.

## This Is Not Normal Bro

You don't need anyone else.
You just told me all the things you want
and I told you *Good Luck! I want that*
*for you too.* We laughed. We don't need
to spend another twenty years
apart. There was no one else then, or now.
I said, there's no point
in trying to date—you said,
this is the show, again.            The Show.
And we've already tried to be apart, to move
apart, to see all the best in our others, but you
said to me—
*This is not normal, bro—*

how we're faint for each other,
how the dizzy lure never stops,
and how that started.            How did it start?
Our story begins with the doorman for the Waldorf Astoria—
Antony Orlando, and how he drove me
to Parsippany, New Jersey
to your makeshift studio
in your parents' basement
and we bonded across the room
over the records of that time. Then,

we went to a party, and you sat close to me,
smiled, asked me to a show. We had
a nice dinner, a nice time
and then you said we attacked each other.
I don't think it was five blowjobs.
You tend to exaggerate.

And then, we were never apart
till we were
and now
you call me at one-thirty on Christmas morning,
right as your divorce moved into the room,

me calling you back over the years
to tell you that love enduring
is normal. We are as normal as
the doorman getting friend-zoned.

## Recovered Notes in Bird and Lover

I breathe a pirate's sheet of fog when I open my mouth,
and every morning, it fills with faded roses.

Between my legs, sails
and the golden suns of the south.
How much for this quilted, cursing sparrow,
the back of a woman's calves,
the piano-key stutter of daughters
holding the dustpan for pennies—

I am the many that crawl out of the halo of hours.
We are a sunken couch filled with marvel,

the light fixtures our heads like grist,
the moor of your forehead on the tip of my chin.

What is music to a woman
if not recovered notes in bird and lover.

## Night on Earth

Who can know
what marriage of palettes,

what injured
blue with green,

who sold ash to gold?
Who fell for whom first?

Who loved
the most when?

We have stars
under our fingernails

to scratch and fasten the light
in this bowl of night
          turned upside
down.

# ACKNOWLEDGMENTS

I would like to thank the people who work for the complete and total freedom of all women.

*The Abandoned Playground:* "Gratitude Poem with Swimming" and "What to Do with the Brutes"
*Cortland Review:* "Pandemic Romance Dream During a Sunrise Hurricane"
*Dead Mule School of Southern Literature:* "Bright Life, Animal Heart" and "Cambodian Snake Wine"
*Heavy Feather Review:* "Big Dick, Small Town, I Love You, Now Show Me Your Tits" and "Ghost Ocean"
*Kalliope:* "Dinner Party"
*The Lincoln Review:* "Black Clothes in a Pile," "Gratitude Poem for One of Us," and "Neighbor Held Captive Spirals, Stabs Boyfriend Four Times"
*Lungfull Magazine:* "Libidinous Cherry"
*Nelle:* "Cousin Pam & the Want Ads," "Three Girls," and "Witch, Hag, Crone"
*Poetry Is Currency:* "A Copy of *Diving into the Wreck*" and "The Talented Rapes of Our Time"
*Sarah Lawrence Review:* "Night on Earth"
*SWWIM:* "Undo"

## ABOUT THE AUTHOR

Laura Minor's *Bright Life, Animal Heart* won the 2023 Minds on Fire Open Book Prize. Her first book of poems, *Flowers as Mind Control,* won the 2020 John Ciardi Poetry Prize. Her work has appeared in *The Missouri Review, Ploughshares, The Cortland Review,* and *North American Review* among others.

## OTHER TITLES FROM CONDUIT BOOKS & EPHEMERA

*Beneath All Water* by Zackary Medlin

*Extremely Expensive Mystical Experiences for Astronauts* by Dara Barrois/Dixon

*Autoblivion* by Trey Moody

*The Art of Bagging* by Joshua Gottlieb-Miller

*Thunderbird Inn* by Collin Callahan

*The Birthday of the Dead* by Rachel Abramowitz

*The World to Come* by David Keplinger

*Present Tense Complex* by Suphil Lee Park

*Sacrificial Metal* by Esther Lee

*The Miraculous, Sometimes* by Meg Shevenock

*The Last Note Becomes Its Listener* by Jeffrey Morgan

*Animul/Flame* by Michelle Lewis